MW01593187

FIX YOUR SOCIAL SECURITY WITH REAL ESTATE

Nolan Sluder

TATE PUBLISHING, LLC

DEDICATION

This book is dedicated to my two daughters
and their husbands,
Patricia Ann Jones and her husband, Bob
Kimberly Lynn Pool and her husband, Randy
and to my four precious grandchildren,
Nolan Ryan Pool
Rachel Renee Pool
Randall Reed Pool
and
Melody Meade.

ACKNOWLEDGEMENTS

I shall ever be indebted to Anna Bastounes for her untiring effort in working with me to produce this book in the best form possible. I sincerely appreciate her editing and assistance with proper grammar. Anna has arranged my thoughts and content to make them flow in a desirable and readable sequence. I could not have accomplished the quality of *Fix Your Social Security with Real Estate* without Anna's help.

I greatly appreciate the patience and support of my dear wife, Millie. The encouragement of those I have mentored and helped on their way to Biblical prosperity has given me the willpower and determination to finish this book.

TABLE OF CONTENTS

PART I
THE FOUR GIANTS OF REAL ESTATE INCOME

PART II
THE BARGAIN PROPERTY—YOUR KEY TO SUCCESS

FOREWORD

The Social Security System that was designed to help Americans is now in need of help to survive.

By inspiration and experience, Nolan Sluder offers hope and help to Americans for their financial security. For many years, Nolan Sluder has demonstrated an ability to acquire and market residential properties. He has also trained others how to be successful in real estate. His high energy level and enthusiasm have motivated hundreds of people to take charge of their financial future.

As Nolan's banker and friend for over 15 years, I have personally observed his success and admired his willingness to help others in all areas of life.

You will have taken a step toward your future financial security by reading, and using the principles and methods in this book. This is not a get-rich-quick plan. It is a common sense approach to a successful real estate business.

Randy L. Smith
Executive Vise President
Citizens State Bank
Tyler, Texas

INTRODUCTION

Perhaps you've picked up this book because you are intrigued by its title and by the prospect of "fixing" your social security retirement plan. Experts tell us that not too many years from now, the government Social Security system will be in the red, paying out more than it takes in. For many young Americans, the prospect of paying into a system from which they will likely receive few or no benefits is not a bright one. Your Creator never intended for you to become the victim of a failed government program.

I'm old enough to remember when the United States Congress passed the 1935 Social Security Act. The novel idea of paying into a fund that would provide a supplemental income to aging Americans seemed like a good idea at the time. I believe it still is today. Remember, Social Security payments were never meant to be one's sole source of income back in the thirties, nor are they meant to be that today. Yet, millions of seniors anxiously await the arrival of a government check each month because for them, it means survival. Worse yet, scores of younger Americans are not planning for their retirement. It doesn't take a genius to see a crisis in the making.

Young or old, I don't think we should be the objects of political maneuvering. While the politicians try to rescue a failing system, I want to show you how to be free from anxiety, never again to worry about any Social Security check you might receive. You *can* reach a place of financial security you never dreamed possible.

The idea of planning for abundant income during my senior years did not occur to me when our elected officials began sounding the alarm about an impending crisis. Rather, I was in my thirties when I determined to take control of my financial future. I did this by using the one tool that has worked so well for American families for many generations. Real estate is that tool.

Through trial and error, over nearly 50 years, I have learned what works and what does not work in the real estate business. At this time in my life, I'm consumed with a desire to help younger people make right choices and take right actions to secure a better financial future for themselves and for their families. Real estate has secured the hard-earned savings of many American families. It is a safe haven for your money in both good times and bad.

It is important you reject the preconceived idea that real estate will not work for you. You *can* be successful in planning your financial future. Great fortunes are made and sustained in real estate. I believe you, too, can succeed if you take the following steps.

BUILD ON PRINCIPLES

There are two principles that are absolutely necessary for success. The first is determination. You must make up your mind and be resolute in your conviction that God's plan for you is to prosper. Second, you must be persistent. This means you continue to work this plan even in the face of opposition or interference.

ACQUIRE KNOWLEDGE

You must have knowledge to proceed. I wrote this book to supply you with that knowledge. The information and "how-to" directions contained in this book can change your life. Diligently study to understand the methods set forth in these pages. Study them again and again. They *will* produce results, but the decision to put them into practice is yours to make.

DEVELOP SKILLS

Skill comes through practice. Initiate a real estate deal by purchasing a bargain property and you'll be on your way. With each transaction, come skills to make wiser decisions about future investments. You learn by doing.

It is my personal prayer that you will study and apply these wealth-building principles. If you do, you will succeed in realizing your financial dreams.

A great step in realizing that dream is to understand what money is all about.

WHAT IS MONEY?

- MONEY is bread when you are hungry.
- MONEY is the transportation that takes you where you want to go.
- MONEY is a generous offering or gift when you are confronted with a need in God's kingdom or a desire to help an unfortunate friend.
- MONEY is substance with which to build or buy a comfortable home for you and your family.
- MONEY is a well-furnished table when you wish to have family or friends over for dinner.

- MONEY is the service of the best doctor or medical help when your health fails.
- MONEY is a generous basket of groceries and other supplies for a needy family at Christmas time.
- MONEY is the tuition for your children and grandchildren to get the best education available.
- MONEY is the fuel to keep your home warm on the coldest day or night.
- MONEY is the power to light your home and run all the appliances that make housekeeping and home life convenient.
- MONEY is the inheritance you wish to leave to your children and grandchildren when you depart this life and go to be with God.
- MONEY is all this and more.
- MONEY is to be respected; not loved or worshipped.
- MONEY is to be your servant, not your master.
- MONEY must always be acquired honestly. However, it is necessary that you do acquire it!
- To waste MONEY is sinful and foolish.
- To manage MONEY well and cause it to increase is a virtue.
- Don't spend a lifetime working for MONEY.
- LEARN NOW how to put MONEY to work

for you.
- MONEY is a great employee!
- MONEY is waiting for you to put IT to work
  AS YOUR SLAVE.

Nolan Sluder
Tyler, Texas

CHAPTER 1

HOW I DISCOVERED THE POWER OF
REAL ESTATE
TO CREATE WEALTH

As a teenager during the Great Depression, I was intrigued when I listened to the conversations of men who bought and sold real estate during that very difficult time. What struck me was the hope and purpose I saw in them. While despair gripped millions of Americans, these men spoke enthusiastically about their successes and optimistically about the future. In my mind, the contrast couldn't have been sharper. Those conversations left a lasting impression on my young mind.

I loved studying the history of my home state, Oklahoma, when I was a student. The story of the Oklahoma Land Rush captured my attention. The pictures in my history book showed eager settlers lined up, waiting for the signal to rush and claim the very best real estate available. They used whatever form of transportation they had in their quest for a homestead. Those who did not own a horse, wagon or mule, simply ran on foot to stake out their claim to the beautiful Oklahoma real estate. I'll never forget the picture of one very determined man who rode his cow in search of the perfect parcel of land.

My lessons also included the exciting adventures of pioneers who braved the elements and the dangers to travel to such far off lands as California and Alaska. These hearty souls were looking for that special piece of real estate wherein they would find treasures of gold. I assure you there are still great treasures to be found in real estate. In whatever state you call home, wonderful opportunities await you. You can find a fortune in the crown jewel of all investments—real estate.

By the time I was thirty, I had already become a pioneer preacher, planting new congregations in areas where they were most needed. Financially, these were very lean times for my family and me. I searched for a source of steady income that met the needs of my family and let me give my full attention to the ministry. In my search, I discovered real estate.

Now, some fifty years later, my wife and I have owned and rented many single-family homes and approximately one thousand two hundred apartments. The principles and plans contained in this book are those that I put to work for me as I pursued my own financial security. Today, my wife and I have no concern about whether or not the Social Security system is solvent as it applies to our own needs, nor are we worried about our financial future.

Often, when I begin to encourage someone to consider real estate as a source of wealth building, I am met with many objections. Here are three I frequently hear:

"I don't have any money."
(It takes money to make money, right?)

The answer is "Not necessarily." Start where you are with what you have. My wife and I began our married life with $19.50. My salary was $16 a week. The key factor is not how much money you make, but what you do with what you have and with what you receive.

"I don't have time to buy or sell real estate."

It takes no more time to sell a house than it does to sell a car, an appliance or a room full of furniture. The big difference is in the profit you can make. Sell small items and you're looking at profits in the hundreds of dollars. Sell a house and you're now talking about profits in the thousands of dollars.

"I don't know anything
about buying and selling real estate. "

The purpose of this book is to give you the knowledge you'll need to get started. Your knowledge will increase with experience.

Decide this moment to keep an open mind toward what you are about to learn. One of the greatest moments of your life will be the day you make your first successful deal.

In this book, you'll learn about these four giants of real estate income:

1. The Wealth-building Power of Cash Profits from Real Estate Sales
2. The Wealth-building Power of Rental Real Estate
3. The Wealth-building Power of Owner Financing
4. The Wealth-building Power of Equity Growth

Let me show you how these four giants can work for you.

PART I

THE FOUR GIANTS OF REAL ESTATE INCOME

CHAPTER 2

THE WEALTH-BUILDING POWER OF
CASH PROFITS FROM
REAL ESTATE SALES

Buy and sell a bag of peanuts and your profit will be peanuts. Buy and sell a house and your profit will be thousands of dollars.

The simplest way to begin making money in real estate is to buy bargain properties for cash and then resell them at a profit. *What is a "bargain"? Throughout this book, I will use the word "bargain" to describe a property that can be purchased, marked up, and sold for 30% to 50% or more over your cost.*

Certainly, home prices vary greatly from market to market across the nation. A home that sells for $75,000 in a rural community may cost $500,000 in a large, metropolitan area. While this is true, the percentage of profit does not change from one market to another. Remember, when you buy, always look for a bargain.

CIRCUMSTANCES THAT CREATE A BARGAIN

The market value of a property can vary greatly, depending on circumstances influencing the sale. Often, a bargain is created when distressing circumstances demand an immediate sale. Here are a few examples of such circumstances:

- The owner must sell as quickly as possible due to a financial setback, a divorce, the death or illness of a family member, the loss of a job, a transfer by their employer, or other such situations.
- The heirs of an estate want their money, now!
- A mortgage company or bank wants a repossessed property out of its inventory.
- The owner does not know how to solve an existing problem with a property and wants to let someone else deal with it.
- The owner has neglected to make his mortgage payments and is about to lose his property.
- The owner is unaware of the value of his property and for personal reasons sells it at a price below market value.

I have purchased property at extremely low prices under all of the above circumstances. In many cases, I offered less than the distress price and have had those offers accepted.

BUILD A CASH RESERVE

While some may think buying for cash is impossible, it is not. Here are some practical steps you can take to increase the cash you have available to purchase real estate.

• Save your money.

Don't spend all the money you receive. Lay aside a portion of all income for investments. The $20 you save by not eating at a restaurant may seem insignificant. However, it's really like a seed. If you plant it, it will grow. Today, my own saving plan is still what it was years ago. My wife and I put all our income above our living expenses and giving commitments into purchasing real estate.

• Limit credit card use.

Credit cards can be the greatest barrier between you and your financial success. There are three things that spell disaster for the holder of credit cards. First, there is the temptation to use them excessively. Second, is the high interest rate charged on balances that are carried over each month. The final trap is the repayment plan that allows the cardholder to make minimum payments. Determine to pay the entire balance of each credit card bill each month. If you do not have the willpower to limit the use of the card, you must cut it up.

• Stop impulse buying.

Beware of attractive, eye-catching merchandise on display at your local store. If you don't really need an item, don't buy it. Don't buy everything your appetite calls for. Impulse buying will deplete your wallet before you know it. Remember, your cash on hand is the seed that allows you to purchase income-producing property.

• Keep your old car.

Refuse to spend money for a new or different car just for the sake of changing vehicles. Won't you be surprised to see your old car (which you were certain had outlived its usefulness) being driven by the new owner several years after you sold it? Your present car is very likely the most economical one you will ever own.

• Avoid buying expensive gifts.

A simple card or a small cash gift given with love will mean just as much as an expensive gift.

• Shop wisely.

Avoid the temptation to shop at convenience stores. These are great places to waste money. Make a shopping list and do your buying at discount stores. Over time, you will save hundreds of dollars by following this simple rule.

• Pay your debts.

Today's personal bankruptcy rate is higher than it has ever been. According to some estimates, nearly 75% of American households spend 3–4% more than their income. This habit of overspending can lead to financial ruin. Start with the small debts and keep paying until all are cleared. Once you are out of debt, stay out of debt. The only good reason to borrow money is for the purpose of making more money.

• Prioritize your time.

Don't waste your free time. Use it to learn and earn. Study the principles contained in this book and you will enhance your income-producing potential. Use your time to discover new ways to earn additional income.

• Take a second job.

A second job is a great way to get a head start on your way to financial freedom. Seek to save the entire amount of your second paycheck in addition to your other savings. One of my students, a university graduate, mowed lawns in order to earn money for the down payment on his first property.

BE A CREATIVE CASH BUYER

If you do not have enough cash on hand to buy a bargain-priced house, then consider making your first two or three real estate deals in the following manner:

Put a small down payment on a house and finance the balance. Do whatever is necessary to improve your bargain so that you can sell it for top dollar. Sell the house for cash and pay off the mortgage. Use the profit to buy a second house. Repeat these steps until you build a substantial cash reserve. After two or three cash deals you should have $40,000 to $50,000 on hand to make your first cash purchase.

Where do you get financing? There are several sources. You can approach a mortgage company or credit union. My advice is to develop a relationship with a local banker to whom you can go for your first loan and for additional funding down the road. If you have the cash for a modest down payment, you should have no problem getting financing for your investment property. Perhaps a family member or friend will loan you money to buy property. You should pay them interest just like you would a bank.

In 2002, a friend of mine bought her first house for $16,000 using $9,000 in cash along with a $7,000 cash advance she secured with a credit card. In three days, she sold the house for $32,000, using owner financing for the sale. She collected mortgage payments for 18 months before deciding to sell the note for $22,500. Approximately $9,200 from the down payment and mortgage payments was received by that time. After paying her credit card and deducting the amount of her cash investment, her profit was approximately $14,000 after expenses. Remember, she had no previous real estate experience. While I am not a great believer in the use of credit cards, I do believe there are times they can be used to make a handsome profit.

CHAPTER 3

THE WEALTH-BUILDING POWER
OF RENTAL REAL ESTATE

For those who may have doubts about the ownership of rental real estate, consider this:

The house you buy and rent for twenty years will more than double in value because of inflation. It may even triple in price in some areas. The house will have paid for itself at least two times within those twenty years. When you sell the house, finance it yourself and collect monthly payments for twenty or more years. Clearly, rental property has great potential to increase your income.

Cash brought in by rent and lease payments from properties you own can be a major source of revenue for your retirement. When you own a rental property, you allow others (tenants) to pay for your property. This leaves you with a free and clear deed. The wealth-building dynamics of rental real estate can be an important tool in securing your family's material well being.

USE THESE SEVEN KEYS WHEN PURCHASING RENTAL REAL ESTATE

1. Choose a location where rental units are in demand.
2. One way to determine whether there is a demand in an area is to check the classified ads in the local newspaper. If you find an abundance of rental units in a particular area, you are wise to consider a different location. Seeing several vacancy signs on rental properties in an area should lead you to the same conclusion. You may want to call several apartment complexes to check on vacancy   rates. Simply put, avoid areas where there is evidence of more vacancies than tenants seeking housing.
3. Consider how much work and expense you will incur in preparing the property to be rented.
4. If you are buying a duplex or apartment building, be sure there is ample and convenient parking for the tenants.
5. Figure your expenses. These include property taxes, insurance premiums, and utilities. If you hire a manager, this will also be an additional expense.
6. If there is evidence of unrest or dissatisfaction among the current tenants of a property, discuss

this with the present owner.

7. Determine whether or not your purchase will be profitable. Look at the ratio between the gross rent per month and the price you are paying for the property.

If you pay $60,000 for a rental property, the monthly rent should be no less than $900. If you pay $40,000, the monthly rent should be no less than $600. This is called the "ratio-of-rent-to-cost" of the property. The monthly rental income should never be less than one and one-half percent of the cost of the property. Any amount of rent more than one and one-half percent per month just makes it better. At two percent, the rent on a $60,000 property should be $1,200.

When you borrow the money to purchase rental property, I recommend you pay off the mortgage as soon as possible. Anytime you pay off a mortgage early, your savings will be enormous. Well-managed free and clear rental property has never failed to increase the wealth of the owner.

OWN AND MANAGE REAL ESTATE

You can hire a company to manage your rentals for you. This will reduce your cash flow, but it is an option if you want less personal involvement. A charge of fifteen percent of the rental rate is the norm for most management companies.

• Advertising

Newspaper ads are a good source for tenants. When you place a classified ad, use such descriptive words as nice, clean, and spacious in the ad. Design your newspaper ads to get telephone calls. Don't put all the details in the text because the purpose of the ad is to get people to call you. Give the details in person once you have set up a time to show the apartment or house.

Most want ads are placed in alphabetical order. For example, if you begin your ad with the letter "a", it will most likely be the first listing in the rental section of the paper. You might use, "A Better Place to Live" as the opening line of your ad.

Put the amount of monthly rent in your ad. People looking for rentals usually have a certain budget limit. When I see an ad without a price, I assume the price is very high. Some owners mistakenly think price listings scare away prospective tenants. I ignore ads that do not list the selling price.

• The Security Deposit

Don't put the amount of the security deposit in the ad. If I'm asked about the deposit, I simply say, "Let's meet and we can talk about the security deposit. Our rates are very reasonable." Don't commit yourself in an ad or on the telephone to a deposit amount. It is better to meet the prospective tenant and then decide on the security deposit amount.

Always let tenants know your expectations with regard to cleanliness, noise level, parking rules, etc. Never move a tenant into a dirty apartment or house. This gives him an excuse to ask for the deposit back when he vacates the premises without cleaning it properly. It's best to use a checklist that both the tenant and landlord sign at the time the unit is rented.

• Signs

Use signs to keep your houses and apartments full. I don't advise putting a "For Rent" sign on the property itself. This signals a vacancy. A house or apartment that is visibly empty is an invitation to vandals. It's a good idea to keep the blinds closed or the drapes drawn as if every unit was full. Never show all the vacant units. When a prospective tenant comes to see an apartment, show him only one unit even if others are vacant. If you show all the vacant units, the renter may think something is wrong with the apartment complex.

Showing all your vacant units takes away the prospective tenant's sense of urgency. He'll think he has plenty of time to shop around before getting back to you.

Place medium or small signs near busy locations. One of my signs reads: Luxury, one-bedroom apartment for rent. Call (903) XXX-XXXX. A sign will generate calls.

If you operate a fair and equitable business and care for your tenants, you will build up a clientele. You'll be surprised at the number of calls you receive when prospects need a rental apartment or house.

• Lease and Rental Agreements

It is not necessary to mention a lease in your ad. You can require it when the prospective renter agrees to take the apartment or house. I don't use leases because I want the option of asking an undesirable tenant to move. Also, if the tenant is unhappy, he has the option to move. I don't like dealing with unhappy people every month. Instead of a lease, I use a good rental agreement that sets forth the rental rate, the amount of the damage and clean up deposit, the responsibilities of both tenant and landlord, and the amount of late payment charges. Be sure the agreement states that a tenant who moves out before a certain period loses his security deposit.

Supply each tenant with a smoke alarm. Get a written receipt from tenant, which verifies the alarm was received in good, working order.

The rental business is not a welfare business. Always keep the relationship between you and the tenant businesslike. When you do, the tenant will know you expect your payments on time and expect him to take good care of the property.

From time to time, you'll meet people whose stories will tug at your heartstrings. I prefer to operate my real estate business at a maximum profit and then give offerings and donations from the money I earn.

There may be times when you want to bless your tenants. At Christmas, I often show my appreciation to my tenants by reducing their December rent by $25, $50, or $75.

BUILD NEW RENTALS

If you decide to build rentals, there is much to consider. When you build with cash, you will be committing that cash for several months before ever seeing a return. It can take from three to five months to prepare the ground, start the construction, and finish a building that's ready to be rented.

When you borrow the money to build, this increases your building expense because of the interest you will pay on the interim loan. This is the loan you acquire for the building project. You then have the additional expense of setting up the permanent financing for the finished building. I suggest you start small, building one home or a few units. The income you receive from these will create the capital you need for future expansion.

If you build apartments, consider one-bedroom or two-bedroom units. If you build three-bedroom apartments, you will attract tenants with large families. In my opinion, garden-type apartments with parking near the door are desirable to most tenants.

TAKE ON A SMALL HOUSE PROJECT

Here is one of my favorite approaches to building income property. Build small, single-family dwellings (approximately 1200 square feet or smaller). If you must go to the bank or mortgage company to finance your property, the small house approach is the easiest way to get financing.

Build the houses on small parcels with individual deeds so you can sell any one house at any time. Rent the houses until they have paid for themselves. Then sell them with owner financing. In this way, you are actually "selling them twice." The first "sale" is the monthly income you receive from renters who eventually move on and leave you with a free and clear property. The second "sale" comes when you sell the property with owner financing and collect payments for many years. When looking for a buyer for your rental property, don't forget the current renter. Often, he is your best prospect

BUILD A MOBILE HOME PARK

Another great rental project is a mobile home park. The first thing you need to do is to secure a building site. Don't start with less than five acres. It is better to start with fifteen acres or more. I have done this more than once. Check to see if you need permits. Be sure water service is available. If a sewer line is not available, check to see how much space you'll need for the septic systems.

Building a mobile home park gives you the advantage of building it one space at a time. The income from the first spaces built will pay for the next spaces. In other words, the mobile home park actually builds itself. One park with fifty or more spaces will provide a handsome retirement.

PURCHASE AN EXISTING MOBILE HOME PARK

Look for a mobile home park that is fully occupied, clean, and well maintained. Be sure to avoid overcrowded parks. Always check for sewer problems before buying. When making your purchase, use the following income-to-sales-price ratio: A monthly income of $6,000 will justify a $300,000 purchase price. Several factors can cause these figures to vary a bit. These include location, the age of the mobile homes occupying the park, and the potential for rental increases. Get an appraisal of the park. However, I advise you not to pay the appraised price. Just be sure the monthly rental income is two or three percent of the cost per space. Let me clarify. If you pay $300,000 for a 50-space park, you are paying $6,000 per space. The rental for each space should be at least $120. If your cost per space is $10,000, then your rent should be at least $200 per month for each space.

PAY AS YOU GO

You can reach a level of operating your rental business with cash much sooner than you think. To do so takes discipline, planning, and self-denial. You must be willing to avoid debt and pay-as-you-go.

Debt and reckless spending are monsters that devour your income. They will keep you awake at night and make you sick. On the other hand, money saved, wisely invested and managed well will increase and provide the abundance your Creator intended for you and your family.

Remember begin where you are with what you have. If you need to use the bank's money to get started, do so. Always keep your debt at a manageable level. Keep your monthly payments well inside your ability to meet your obligations. Keep a comfortable reserve on hand. Good business practices pay great dividends.

CHAPTER 4

THE WEALTH-BULDING POWER OF OWNER FINANCING

Buying homes and selling them to families through owner financing is probably the easiest and fastest way to create wealth for your personal financial security.

Owner financing is simply a financial arrangement in which you, as the seller of a property, take the place of a financial institution and become the lien holder.

In this book, I'll use figures from transactions in the East Texas area to illustrate the power of real estate to create wealth. While prices vary from one geographic region to another, the profit percentages should be similar in other areas of the United States.

Consider the following scenario:

You buy a bargain property for $45,000 cash and sell it for $69,800 using owner financing. You collect a $7,000 down payment. The terms of the note call for the $62,800 balance to be paid at a rate of $585 per month including 8.4% interest. At this rate, the note will be paid in 199 months. You paid $45,000 for the property. You will receive a total of $123,415 (down payment plus mortgage payments). Your profit will be $78,415.

You can take the $62,800 note to your banker as security for a loan. Give him an assignment on it, and request a loan for your next deal. Use that loan to buy a second bargain. You resell it and now have two note payments coming in each month and only one payment going out. You may, very soon, have the cash to purchase your third bargain.

Owner financing opens a whole new avenue of possibilities. There are many prospective buyers who are willing to buy and fix up a house in order to reach their goal of home ownership. Every dollar they spend and every hour they labor improving the house greatly increases the value of your security.

When you arm yourself with knowledge and manage your affairs well, your financial growth is indeed awesome. Is there effort to put forth? Does is require good money management? It certainly does, but the rewards make the effort worthwhile.

You will receive the highest market price for properties that are sold on terms that make the purchase easy and convenient for the buyer. Solve a buyer's problem and your financial reward will be great.

LEARN THE TOP TEN SECRETS OF OWNER FINANCING

1. You are in charge.

You choose the location of your security because you choose where you buy property. Don't buy a property based upon where you would like to live. Rather, choose houses that will sell in your market area. Whatever sells is what you are looking for.

You also choose when you buy. Always remember to be patient when looking for your bargain. Don't get anxious and spend too much for investment property.

You set the cost of the property. How do you do this? You do this by making an offer. Forget the listed price. Offer the amount you are willing to pay, not the amount the seller wants to receive. Don't be afraid to negotiate. Over time, your negotiation skills are sure to improve.

A few years ago, I found a property for sale for $25,000. I quickly made a $13,000 offer on it. Now it took a few days for the broker and seller to get over the shock of my low offer, but the day came when I received a phone call and heard the words, "We accept."

I sold the house four hours later for $29,500. The $12,000 I saved on the purchase price certainly made a great difference. Don't forget, you are in charge.

You choose the buyer. You are not obligated to sell to anyone. When you have a good feeling about a person and are confident of his or her ability to pay, you can then set terms to meet the needs of the buyer.

The best place for me to close a real estate deal is sitting at my computer. The amortization program on my computer is the best selling tool I have. When I'm in the field, selling a property, I tell the prospective buyer, "Come over to my office and let me show you how long it will take you to pay for this house." I use my amortization program to set out various payout scenarios, showing the amount of the monthly payments needed for a 10, 15, or 20-year loan.

I think a fair interest rate for owner-financed property is 2 or 3 percentage points above the going rate for a bank loan. If banks are charging 6.5% for home loans, then feel free to charge between 8.5% to 9.5% interest on your owner-financed properties. By purchasing from you, the buyer saves money on closing costs and does not have to undergo the rigor-ous loan approval process required by a bank. By all means, be sure you operate in a manner that allows you to go home and sleep at night. Buyers may be willing to pay extra interest, but they don't want to deal with someone who'll gouge them.

2. You set the monthly payment.

You set the monthly payment and the grace period in which a payment can be made without a late charge. I choose ten days. You can set any time period you like. By law, late charges cannot exceed 5% of the monthly payment amount.

I want my buyers to pay out their notes, so I structure the notes accordingly. I have never set up a deal that I wanted to come back to me. Yet, I have never repossessed a property that I did not sell for more money than was owed against it. Over the years, I have had only a 2–3% repossession rate.

3. You collect interest on your cost of the property and your profit.

The amount of an owner-financed note is the balance owed to you after the down payment has been made. The amount includes your invest-ment (cost) and your profit. The interest received on owner-financed notes is figured on both the investment and the profit.

4. You decide how and when you'll be taxed by the IRS.

You have at least two options when it comes to paying income taxes on the profits made from owner-financed properties. One option calls for you to pay all income taxes in the year of the sale of a property. For example, if you buy a property for $20,000 and sell it for $39,500, you can pay taxes on the $19,500 profit at one time. This way, you won't pay taxes on the subsequent principle payments.

However, you also have the option of spreading out the taxes on your profit over the life of the note. You do this by using a "ratio-of-profit" formula. For example, if you buy for $20,000 and sell for $40,000, you have a 50% ratio-of-profit factor. You arrive at this figure by dividing the profit by the selling price. By exercising this option to pay your income taxes over the life of the note, this allows you to generate capital to buy more property.

Your own personal circumstances in any given year will determine which one of these choices is best for you.

5. You have the option of selling your note for cash.

There are mortgage companies and individuals who will buy your owner-financed note for cash. The cash paid for owner-financed notes ranges from 75% to 95% of the face value.

The longer you hold the note, the higher percentage amount you will get for the note. The length of time you hold a note is called "seasoning." A two-year-old note will bring more than a six-month-old note. A note held for five or more years is considered fully seasoned and should yield the highest percentage of cash at the time it is sold.

It's difficult to sell a note that you've held less than a year. It's better to let your notes season a little because note buyers look at the consistency of payment and age of a note when determining the amount they will pay for it.

What percentage can you expect when you sell a note for cash? It depends on the economic times. When interest rates are low, the price paid for owner-financed notes is high. A few years ago, I received a letter from a New York note buyer. In the margin of his letter, he included a handwritten note that read: "I will pay up to 102% for your note." In order to receive a high percentage for your note, it must be well secured and seasoned. The interest rate must be high and the payment record consistent.

6. You can donate your note to your church or favorite charity and receive a tax deduction in return.

If you donate an owner-financed note to a charitable organization, you can have the price of the note deducted from your taxable income.

7. You can minimize your expense of doing business by closing your real estate deals yourself.

Although I do this, I do not recommend it to you. If you plan to close your own deals, be sure to consult an attorney in the state where you are doing business.

You may want to take a real estate law class in order to learn the procedures and documents needed for real estate transactions.

8. You can earn more money by depositing owner-financed note payments into a savings account.

As a young man, I had a difficult time saving money. My in-laws were savers. They would put their money into a postal savings account, which, at the time, paid 2% interest. They did this every payday.

I began to save, too. But, every time I put $25 or $30 aside, I saw something I wanted. Too often, I took the money out of my account and spent it. I soon figured that my best hope for saving was to make money in lump sums. No matter how you earn your money, you need a plan to save it. The following illustration demonstrates the potential of consistent saving.

You purchase a bargain property for $13,000. You sell the property for $29,500 and receive a $1,000 down payment. The terms of the note call for the balance of $28,500 to be paid over a fifteen year period at $306 per month at 10% interest. If every payment is deposited into a savings account which averages 5% interest, the balance at the end of fifteen years will be approximately $82,000.

Savings is a mighty engine that works in your favor. Your $28,500 note is earning 10% interest. When you put the monthly payments into a savings account, you earn interest on your interest as well as on the principle. As you continue on this course, the interest you draw at the bank earns interests as well.

However, this is not the end of the story. Let's call this deal "NOTE #1."

9. You can reinvest the income from owner-financed notes and receive an enormous harvest of cash.

After saving the payments on NOTE #1 for four years, you will have approximately $16,000 in your savings account. Take the $16,000 and purchase another bargain property. Resell it for $29,500, using similar terms as you did for NOTE #1. We'll call this NOTE #2. You now have two notes which are adding about $612 per month to your account. If you allow the money to remain in the account, you will have $147,800 by the time NOTE #2 is paid out. This happens just nineteen years after you made your initial $12,000 investment. What a picture of the awesome power of owner financing and a well-managed savings plan.

Certainly, the rate of savings will vary as interest rates vary. But, in any case, saving money received from owner-financed notes is a disciplined way to build cash resources.

10. You decide when to make more money.

You set your income. You can work as hard as you want in this business. You can buy as many houses as you can find at bargain prices.

I highly recommend selling your properties with owner financing. It gives you the best of all phases of the real estate business. You are the buyer, the seller, and the banker.

One of the greatest hurdles in starting a business is acquiring start up capital. Through the use of real estate, the income you receive after expenses becomes the capital you use for future purchases.

When you reinvest your profits back into more income-producing property, your rate of growth is staggering.

CHAPTER 5

THE WEALTH-BUILDING POWER OF
EQUITY GROWTH

Equity accumulation is a wealth-building tool that often goes unnoticed. Every month, homeowners build the silent financial asset of home equity when they make their house payment. Mortgage companies and banks know this. That is why they spend thousands of dollars for advertising to lure the homeowner into pledging that equity for a loan. The finance company knows the homeowner will soon spend the equity loan. When the money is gone, more equity will be built up. The finance company gets to make another loan and reaps more interest.

I want to help you become money smart. You can put this powerful "equity-growth" engine to work building your wealth. This engine works wonders when applied to income-producing properties in the following three ways:

1. The depreciation you take on rental property reduces your taxes.

2. The property gains value because of inflation.
3. The tenant pays your mortgage and gives you cash to spend.

What better investment could you ask for?

MY PERSONAL EXPERIENCE WITH EQUITY GROWTH

Equity growth is not always visible when you own a property. Let me explain. In the early 1960s, my wife and I bought a new house in Mesa, Arizona. After living in it for nearly 11 years, we sold the house for more than double what we paid for it. Our monthly payments had reduced the mortgage, property values had gone up, and we reaped a harvest of equity growth.

From Mesa, we moved to Tyler, Texas where we found a colonial-style home surrounded by 19 acres. The deal included mineral rights, two guesthouses, and approximately one-half mile of road frontage. By the way, there is a small fishing lake just 100 yards behind the house. It was bargain priced at $62,000 with owner financing. When I found the property, did I hesitate? Did I sleep on it? I certainly did not. It took me all of fifteen minutes to write an earnest money check, sign the contract, and purchase the property. Don't be indecisive and wait too long when a good bargain comes your way.

An oil company drilled a well on our land and struck oil. The royalties we received paid our entire mortgage. Today, both our married daughters have homes on the land. The colonial house and the few acres it occupies is now worth more than four times what I paid for the entire property. Equity growth will bring you great returns if you give it the chance to do so.

There are many investment options available today. Among them are CDs, 401(k)s, stocks, bonds, and mutual funds. Certainly, these provide handsome returns. However, when you consider the cash profits, rental income, owner-financed note income, and equity growth, I think you'll see why I call real estate the "crown jewel" of all investments.

PART II

THE BARGAIN—YOUR KEY TO SUCCESS

CHAPTER 6

THE HUNT—*FINDING YOUR BARGAIN*

Once again, a bargain is a property that can be purchased, marked up, and sold for 30% to 50% or more than it cost. Always remember, what you pay for a house has nothing to do with what it is worth.

Never pay the retail price for real estate you intend to rent or resell. I'm often asked by brokers, "How much are you looking to spend?" I normally answer, "Well, it depends on what I get for what I'm spending."

Before long, the broker learns that I'm looking for a bargain and I do not want to pay market price. You make your money when you buy the property. This is true because you always buy bargains.

LOOK FOR BARGAIN PROPERTIES

• Look in the classified section of your local paper.

Words like "must sell" or "relocating" indicate the owner's eagerness to sell the home quickly.

In this circumstance, he may be willing to negotiate the price. When answering classified ads, remember, "The early bird gets the worm." Call immediately when you find a listing for a bargain-priced home.

• Build relationships with local brokers and real estate agents.

Let them know you're always on the look out for a bargain. Ask for referrals from the ones who buy your property.

• Use the Internet.

You can easily search for listings by price and by location. You can also find house auctions and foreclosure listings.

• Contact your county clerk.

Ask if a list of foreclosed homes in your area is posted at the county courthouse. If so, learn the bidding procedure for these bargains.

• Contact the county tax assessor.

Ask about "struck off" properties available for sale. These properties are often sold for the amount of back taxes owed to the county.

• Drive the neighborhood.

An often-overlooked method for finding bargains is simply driving through the neighborhood in which you would like to buy a home. You'll be surprised how many homes you'll find this way.

SEARCH FOR THE BEST BARGAINS

• A House With Extra Land

One of the best purchases you can make is a house located on a large piece of land. The extra land can be built upon or parceled out so it generates large profits for you. Let me share a personal illustration of this principle.

Some years ago, I purchased a house in Tempe, Arizona. The building sat on the corner of a one-acre lot. There were streets on two sides of the property. This configuration gave me a good-sized lot on each street outside the perimeter of the land occupied by the house.

Instead of selling the house, I rented it. The rent payments more than covered my mortgage payments. I hired a surveyor to survey "out" the house. This separated it from the rest of the land tract. The empty land was now mine. I owned it free and clear.

I went to another mortgage company and borrowed money to build a four-unit apartment on each of the two lots. When the buildings were completed, I had a total of nine rental units on the property. I held this property and received the rental payments for many years. When I finally decided to sell the property, it produced income for me for another 12 to 15 years through owner financing.

As you hunt for your bargain, look for a home with extra land. It has the potential to produce more revenue.

• Properties with two or more residences

Obviously, a property with a home, an extra apartment, or a multi-family dwelling like a duplex or triplex will significantly increase your income.

• A "Sleeper" Property

A "sleeper" property is one that the owner has had for a long time. When the owner decides to sell the property, he puts it on the market based upon what he paid for it many years before. When you find a sleeper, buy it immediately. If you don't, someone else will. Don't let a sleeper sleep too long.

I learned a lesson about sleepers all too well when I first moved to Tyler, Texas. The day I arrived in town, I saw a four-acre piece of land at the corner of a busy intersection. A fire-damaged house was on the property. The sale price was $89,000. I knew it was a bargain. I made an offer on the property, but in my offer I foolishly included a $10,000 note on an Arizona property. The owners weren't interested in out-of-state notes, so my offer was rejected. I let the deal slip through my fingers. Seven years later, the land sold for one million dollars.

Was I disappointed? Sure, but I didn't look back. You must always look ahead. You will miss a good deal once in a while. Just go on your way and begin the hunt for another bargain.

• A property that can be purchased from the owner

It is often easier to negotiate an offer directly with an owner. The reason for this is the owner doesn't have to pay a commission to a broker if he sells the property himself.

• A distress or emergency sale

A family emergency or crisis can sometimes require the quick sale of a piece of property. Under such circumstances, the selling price is usually set below market value. You get to purchase the property at a bargain price, and the seller is satisfied with the quick sale. It's a win-win situation for all parties.

Certainly, foreclosures fit into this category. Foreclosed homes are often listed with real estate brokers. Mortgage companies and government agencies like HUD list their foreclosures with brokers. These homes normally sell below market value.

One creative way to purchase a home about to be repossessed is to offer to pay for the owner's relocation expenses in exchange for a deed to the property being foreclosed. The owner benefits because he avoids a foreclosure, and you will benefit because your investment is quite small. A word of caution: It's very important to contact the mortgage company before making any arrangements. Be sure you have permission to pay all back payments and assume the mortgage. Contact a lawyer or a title company to be sure you get a title policy on the home. Also, request a Warranty Deed. This will transfer the property to your name.

CHOOSE THE LOCATION

Here's a good rule of thumb: It's better to buy a bad house in a good location, than it is to buy a good house in a bad location. A house in poor condition in a good neighborhood will increase in value just as soon as you fix it up. However, a house in good condition which is located in a poor neighborhood will, over time, decrease in value. You'll find it more difficult to rent or to sell.

INSPECT THE PROPERTY

A number of real estate websites have downloadable checklists for use when inspecting a property. Here is a brief list of important things to check.

- Check the roof to see how much "life" is left in it. If the shingles are curling up, or if you see bubbles, you'll probably need to replace the roof within a year.
- Check under the house and look for wet areas. Also, look for signs of termites and rot. If these problems are present, don't let them deter you. These are fixable problems. Many years ago, I paid $10,000 for a home with termite damage. I simply hired a

carpenter to repair the damage, and later sold the house for $28,500.

- Check the attic to be sure that braces or other structural pieces are secure.
- Check for mold or mildew. Use a chlorine solution to clear these problems.
- Check for soft or uneven places in the floor. These can be fixed, but know that structural repairs such as leveling are costly.
- Check for rotten windowsills, peeling paint, foundation cracks, or cracks in the brickwork.
- Check the heating and air conditioning units.
- Check the septic system.

Be sure to consider these things before making your offer. Every negative factor is a legitimate reason to reduce your offer. Discuss the problem areas with the seller, and then make your offer.

You'll save money if you learn how to fix these problems yourself. However, if you cannot do the repairs, find a good handyman who can handle the minor repairs for you.

If you are not satisfied with the access you have in order to inspect a bargain property, make sure that you make your purchase contingent upon your receipt of a professional inspection report.

CHAPTER 7

THE PURCHASE—BUYING YOUR BARGAIN

Soon after I discovered the income potential of buying and selling real estate, I made a poor real estate decision that left me $10,000 in debt. For me, taking bankruptcy was not an option. My failure was caused by a lack of knowledge. I came very close to quitting, but I corrected my errors and proceeded to pay all who had extended credit to me. Within twelve months, the slate was clear. Looking back, I realize that quitting would have been a very tragic mistake. That experience was the first time I lost money in a real estate deal—and it was the last time. Here's the reason why:

As I prayerfully analyzed the errors I had made, three guiding principles came to my mind. I learned the principles well and have practiced them ever since. Together, I call them a "three way safety net".

WEAVE A THREE-WAY SAFETY NET

1. Buy property at a price that would make it possible for you to sell it the very next day at a profit. This can happen only if you buy bargain properties. Remember, you make your money when you buy.
2. Purchase a property that produces sufficient income to cover its expenses (mortgage payments, taxes, maintenance insurance, etc.) and that gives you some money left over for your trouble.
3. .Don't exhaust all your resources on the down payment or purchase of a property. At all times, reserve for yourself *cash, collateral, or credit* to use in case of emergency. Good planning and wise decisions will minimize unpleasant "surprises." Remember, the money you have in reserve is still your money.

FUND YOUR PURCHASE

As mentioned earlier, you can buy your bargain with cash, a loan, or by using a credit card. However, it's also a good idea to look for properties that are being sold through owner financing. The interest payment you pay will usually be a few points higher than the going rate, but you eliminate the need to qualify for a bank loan. The important thing to remember is to structure the loan so you can pay it off in as short a time as possible. Whenever possible, make extra principle payments on your mortgage. By all means, pay the loan off quickly. You'll save thousands of dollars over the life of the loan if you do.

GET A CLEAR TITLE

A title policy is simply an owner's insurance policy. The title policy insures you against any defect in the title. By defect, I mean a judgment against the seller. Perhaps there was a divorce and the settlement gave a spouse certain rights if the house was sold. When you get an owner's title policy, you know the title is clear. You can then safely sell the property with a warranty deed.

WORK WITH A BROKER

When you buy a piece of property through a broker, always remember you don't have a commission to pay. The seller pays the commission. It's very good to have a few local brokers working for you if you are the buyer. Their services do not cost you anything. Some of the best deals I've made have come through brokers.

I once called a broker who had a piece of waterfront property listed for $29,500. Because the property needed extensive repair, I offered $16,000 for it. My offer was accepted. The broker gave me excellent service. She was the kind of person who understood that the buyer has the prerogative to make any offer that he sees fit to make.

A few times I've had a broker say to me, "I know my client won't accept your offer." To this, I usually answer, "Where I came from we always let the seller decide whether he wants to take the offer or not." This comment has moved more than one broker into action.

Let brokers know that you are always look-ing for a bargain. They often have bargain pieces of real estate which they want to offer to a responsible cash buyer.

ASK IF THE SELLER IS OPEN TO OFFERS

When dealing with a broker, ask if the seller is open to offers. Listen carefully to the broker's words. Sometimes the broker's words will reveal the owner's eagerness to sell, or the lowest acceptable offer.

One time a broker told me, "Make an offer $10,000.00 below the asking price. These owners want to sell." I made an offer well below the price suggested by the broker. It was accepted. Never be afraid to make a low offer. A knowledgeable broker won't be offended because your offer is lower than the asking price.

CHAPTER 8

THE FIX-UP—*PREPARING YOUR BARGAIN FOR RESALE*

Most of the real good buys are homes that need to be redecorated, renovated, or repaired. Here are a few tips on fixing up your bargain property for resale.

CREATE CURB APPEAL

Curb appeal simply refers to the way a house looks when someone sees it for the first time. First impressions are lasting. One feature I want to emphasize is the front door. The front door is one element than makes a good first impression. A touch of stained glass or side panels on the door can certainly enhance the curb appeal of a home. A few dollars spent on a beautiful front door with glass and brass will pay off handsomely when you put the property up for sale. You can find beautiful doors at discount lumberyards, or even at garage sales. When I find an attractive door, I buy it and put it in storage so I'll have it on hand when I need it.

Landscaping is also an important part of curb appeal. A few dollars spent on flowering plants outside a home will, again, help make a very positive first impression in the mind of a prospective buyer.

DECORATE YOUR BARGAIN

Before you show a house, it must be clean and neat in every way. Make sure the entryway is especially attractive. Give special attention to the kitchen and bathrooms. In my experience, these are the two areas that most concern the wife if you are selling to a couple. Inexpensive blinds and curtains will do much to make the home look more attractive.

When you have to install new flooring and carpeting, don't limit your choices to colors and patterns you like. The same applies to paint colors. Remember, you're not the one who will live in the home. While most people think neutral colors are best, don't be afraid to use vivid colors in your redecorating. These, too, have great appeal to some. A professional paint job will provide a finishing touch like nothing else will.

As you go along, you will develop your decorating skills in making a house attractive to a buyer. Each project will get easier and less expensive.

You'll also enjoy each new challenge a bit more than the last one.

CHAPTER 9

THE RESALE—*SELLING YOUR BARGAIN FOR A PROFIT*

Finding a buyer for your home is really not difficult. There are many buyers for reasonably priced homes. When you consider all the apartments and homes that are being rented, it's clear there's no lack of potential homebuyers. One key is showing these prospective buyers "how" they can purchase a home. This is where owner financing comes in.

MATCH THE HOUSE TO THE BUYER

The cost of houses you will buy to resell will range in price from under $10,000 to approximately $100,000. In all my years of buying real estate, I have worked within this price range. My selling prices have ranged from just under $30,000 to over $160,000. These prices will vary, depending on the area you are in. This great difference in selling prices means you must appeal to the needs of a wide variety of buyers. This makes it necessary to match a buyer to the particular house you are selling. Here are a few examples of this principle in action.

MATCH THE FIX-UP-BUYER TO THE FIX-UP-PROPERTY

There are buyers with carpentry and construction skills who are looking for homes they can fix up. When you acquire a bargain that needs repair, keep the fix-up buyer in mind. When you find him, you'll often make a quick sale and earn a sizeable profit.

One time, I bought a bargain that needed much repair. The land also needed a tremendous amount of clean up. The day I signed the papers and received my deed, I called a friend who had told me he was looking for a "fixer upper." This gentleman and his wife were skilled at making home improvements. They also had friends and family members who were eager to help them. The property cost me just over $13,000. Four hours after the phone call, I showed the couple the property. They eagerly bought it for $29,500. Remember, I did nothing to improve the property. I simply matched the buyer to the property. The buyers removed the trash from the premises, made repairs, and redecorated the home. Today, the property has been appraised for thousands of dollars more than their investment.

MATCH THE READY-TO-MOVE-IN-BUYER WITH A READY-TO-MOVE-IN-HOUSE

It is possible to buy a property at a bargain price that's ready to resell. The only thing needed is the knowledge of how to market the property in order to make the maximum profit.

A beautiful ranch-style, brick home in my community had been on the market for about six months. The sale price was $100,000. The house did not sell. When the broker's listing expired, the owner was very anxious to sell. The owner contacted me because she heard I was a cash buyer. (Note: When you buy a house with your money or with a loan using the bank's money, the owner gets his cash at the close of the sale). I looked at the house and offered $60,000 for it. My offer was accepted. After purchasing the house, I installed an attractive front door and mowed the lawn. In a matter of days, I sold the house for $98,300. I matched a busy, ready-to-move-in buyer with a ready-to-move-in house.

Believe me when I say, there is a buyer for every bargain home that comes into your possession. When people learn you can meet their housing needs, they will be drawn to you like steel pins to a magnet.

Matching buyers with properties makes selling easy. It also results in a happy, satisfied buyer. Some of my best friends are people who've bought houses from me. Learn to match the buyer to the property you have for sale.

SET THE PRICE

Whatever you do, do not under price your house. Regardless of the low price you may have paid for the house, don't pass up the opportunity to make a better than average profit on it. It is more likely you will price it too low than to high. You can always come down a bit, but if your price is too low, you can hardly be successful raising it.

ESTABLISH THE DOWN PAYMENT

When you have an interested buyer, take enough time to visit with him to assess his character and determine his ability to pay. Discuss the amount of the down payment with him. The amount he is currently paying for rent or on a mortgage will indicate the amount he can pay you each month.

I usually try to get at least a 10% down payment. If I'm selling a house for $50,000, I ask for a

$5,000 down payment. If a buyer comes along who wants the house, but has only $3,500, it's time to get creative. In such cases, first ask the party if he expects an income tax refund in the near future. If so, I allow the remaining $1,500 of the down payment to be paid on a specific date after the refund arrives. I include this stipulation in the note.

Another way I allow buyers who lack the entire down payment to purchase a home is to increase their monthly mortgage payments for the first two years of the note. For example, if the monthly mortgage payment is $485 with a $5,000 down payment, then I require a $585 monthly payment when $3,500 is paid down. After the buyer has paid $585 per month for 2 or 3 years, the payment can revert to $485 per month. This, too, must be clearly stated in the written agreement between buyer and seller. There are many different ways you can structure a down payment that will satisfy both buyer and seller.

When structuring a note, be sure to set a realistic monthly payment, which is one that the buyer is capable of handling. It makes life easier for you and for him. You must write all special agreements in the note. Verbal agreements in real estate are not legally binding.

USE THE POWER OF A TRADE

Another way to strike a deal with a prospective buyer is by using a trade. Centuries ago a man named Jacob had a great desire to receive his father's blessing. Esau, Jacob's elder brother, was the rightful heir to this special blessing. Returning home from the field one day, a hungry Esau smelled the aroma of a delicious stew, which Jacob had made. Esau decided to trade his rights, privileges, and the blessing of his father for a portion of Jacob's stew.

I began to learn the power of a trade early in my life. When I began to create income with real estate, I used my trading skills to reach my financial goals. Remember a good trade is one that solves a problem for all parties who are involved in the process.

Here are a few examples of the many trades I've made in real estate:

I found a piece of land for sale in Tempe, Arizona. It was zoned for duplexes. I owned a real estate note on which I was receiving monthly payments. The man who owned the land zoned for duplexes wanted my note. I envisioned ten new duplexes sitting on the property. We traded. He got the note. I got the land. Both of us were satisfied. I obtained financing and built the ten duplexes. The rental income I received from this project more than paid my mortgage payments, taxes, and insurance. In addition, it also gave me a nice, monthly cash flow.

Sometime later, a local schoolteacher wanted the property on which I had built the duplexes. I set a price that would give me a generous profit. The teacher offered a yacht and cash as a down payment. We agreed on the terms and made the trade. Now, I really had no use for a yacht (although I did take it out on the water once for the fun). So, I sold the yacht, made thousands of dollars on the project, paid my taxes, and lived happily ever since. Trading is a wonderful option to consider when putting together real estate deals. Just be sure you make enough profit to justify your trade.

Another time, I acquired a townhouse in one of my trades. I didn't intend to keep the property because there were mortgage payments on it and paying payments was not part of my financial plan. A couple needing a home came to me, but had no cash for the down payment. As we talked they asked if I would consider a trade for the down payment. The lady had a beautiful, expensive mink stole and a 3/4-length mink coat. They offered those beautiful, nearly new minks, valued at $6,000 as a down payment on the townhouse. The stole and coat fit my wife just perfectly. We traded. I got the coats and the couple assumed the mortgage. Both parties were well pleased. Good and fair trades are fun and profitable.

One last example shows the awesome power of a trade. I owned a three-bedroom house free and clear. A friend of mine came to me and asked how he could get started in real estate investing. As we talked, I asked, "What do you have for a down payment?" He showed me a beautiful platinum ring set with two karats of exquisite diamonds. A certified appraisal set the price of the ring at $3,500. We made the trade. I financed the house using owner financing, paid my taxes, and my wife still wears the beautiful ring to this day.

If you will take time to develop and use your trading skills, you will enjoy this profitable activity.

RECOVER YOUR INITIAL INVESTMENT

When structuring a deal, I like to know how long it will take to recover my initial cash investment. A simple way to determine the time it will take to recover your investment is to divide the cost of the property by the amount of the monthly payments.

Let's say you purchase a bargain home for $40,000. You resell it for $70,000, requiring a $7,000 down payment. The balance on the note is payable at a rate of $600 per month at 8.5% interest. At this point, your cost is $33,000 ($40,000 minus the $7,000 down payment). Divide $33,000 (cost) by $600 (monthly payment). This gives you a recovery time of 55 months. The total payout time on the loan is 192 months. Subtract your recovery time (55 months) from the payout time (192 months) and the result is 137 monthly payments—a total of $82,200 over and above your initial investment. When you see a calculation like this one, owner financing becomes *very* attractive.

USE THE BANK'S MONEY

If you are going to use the bank's money to purchase a house for resale, be sure to set the monthly payment from the buyer high enough to pay your monthly obligation at the bank. If the deal is structured properly, your note at the bank will be paid off long before your buyer has paid off the note on the house. The interest you receive will be 2–3 percentage points above what you are paying at the bank. In addition to the small difference in the interest rates, you will make a good profit on the house.

SELL WITH A FIRST LIEN (EVEN IF THE BANK FINANCED YOUR PURCHASE)

Here is a powerful way to remain as the first lien holder on a property which was financed by a bank and which you decide to resell.

You find a bargain property for $40,000. Obtain your purchase money by giving your bank a vendor's lien on the property. Sell the property for $63,500 using owner financing. Collect a $5,000 down payment. You now have a note secured by a vendor's lien in the amount of $58,500. Take the $58,500 note to your bank. Ask your banker to take an assignment on the note in exchange for a release of the original note you gave him when you borrowed you purchase money.

I have done this many times. It's very important to discus this with your banker so that he understands it and will work with you in this manner. If your banker has a problem understanding this principle, you may want to take this paragraph to him.

CHAPTER 10

RETIRE THE EASY WAY

Some of you have decided to use real estate to build your wealth to the highest possible level. Others are looking to use it for a comfortable and sufficient retirement. I am devoting this special chapter to the ones who are thinking only about the retirement benefits of this wonderful concept.

I have a different idea of retirement than many others. To sit in a rocking chair or recliner, allowing my arteries to clog up and my brain to deteriorate has never appealed to me. I suppose the best way to define retirement is "the time of life when you do whatever pleases and fulfills you most." It seems to me that retirement must include financial freedom.

Many people pay into pension plans for retirement. In recent years, we have seen corporate executives using fraudulent accounting practices to steal pension funds which were intended to provide for the retirement of the thousands who paid into the plans.

Now there seems to be a dark cloud hanging over the Social Security system. These circumstances combine to send one message loud and clear: *Do not depend on others to care for your needs as you grow older. Make your plans now to be financially self-sufficient.*

We have already seen the enormous potential of becoming wealthy by practicing the real estate investment principals in this book. Let me now talk specifically about retiring with abundant income to meet your needs during your senior years.

RETIRE WITH RESIDENTIAL UNITS

Begin to acquire rental real estate. Focus on single-family residences, or duplexes and other multi-family units. Set a goal of owning at least eight units. You can hire a manager or you can choose to manage the property yourself. Over the years, I have owned many rentals. I've found great flexibility with rental property. It's not as much trouble as some may think if you keep it in good condition. Apply as much of the rental income as possible to your mortgage payment. In doing so, you will pay your mortgage early and all of the monthly income will then be yours to keep.

If you should decide to build your residential rentals, consider building one house or one duplex at a time. This allows the first rentals built to contribute funds to building the others.

BUILD A RETIREMENT MONEY MAKER

A mobile home park with 50 or more spaces will provide a handsome retirement for years to come. When the first four spaces are built and rented, the income will furnish the capital to finish the project.

USE THE FLEXIBILITY OF RENTAL INCOME UNITS

The time may come when you no longer wish to continue renting your properties. When that happens, you can simply sell your rentals for cash. However, I think you have a better option. Selling your rentals with owner financing will provide a steady income for many years to come. Owner financing also spreads your tax liability over the life of the note.

CHAPTER 11

GETTING STARTED—TAKING YOUR FIRST STEPS

In ancient times, four leprous men sat at the gate of the city of Samaria. The city was under siege by a ruthless and powerful enemy. Food and water were scarce; in fact, most of the people were starving. While their future looked hopeless, the lepers saw it differently. They said to one another, "Why do we sit here waiting to die?" In other words, "We must do something about our situation." They decided to face the enemy head-on, and as a result experienced a great deliverance. I believe there's a lesson for us in this story.

I don't know what our government will finally do to prop up the Social Security system. I do know it would be foolish to sit by and allow a poorly managed government system to ruin your senior years. Here are some steps you can take to get started on your way to the financial security you desire.

• Make a personal financial statement.

This will give you a picture of your current financial condition. For your convenience, a blank form is included at the end of this chapter. I have used this type of financial statement for many years. It has been accepted at the many financial institutions where I've transacted business. Knowing where you are will help you chart the course for your financial future.

• Look for a residential bargain.

When you find a bargain house you will be motivated to find a way to buy it. There is always the possibility the owner will finance it for you. Perhaps you have enough money to pay for it with cash. In any case, find the property first, and then seek for a way to purchase it. Once the deed is in your name, set a selling price and put it on the market. Remember, regardless of how low the purchase price, there is a buyer who will give you top market price for it. You may choose to sell it for cash or with owner financing. Whatever you do, do not set the price too low.

KEEP MOVING FORWARD.

Perhaps you've made your first real estate deal and your profit isn't what you expected. Or, maybe you're struggling to put all the pieces of a real estate deal together. In either case, don't quit. Whatever the situation, you must not quit. You did not start to give up. God created you to be a winner. Your creative ability will manifest itself as you put it into practice. Your profits will increase as you proceed with DETERMINATION and PERISTENCE. With each new deal, you will ACQUIRE KNOWLEDGE and DEVELOP YOUR SKILLS.

The greatest excitement will come when you begin to collect money from your new venture. *When the flow of money starts, remember that more important than the amount of money you receive is what you do with the money you receive.* The way you manage your finances will determine the extent of your success.

First, honor God by giving a tenth of your profit to His work. The remaining money becomes the seed you plant through reinvestment. As you continue down this path, you are on your way to realizing the financial success you have dreamed of.

Always remember, somewhere there is another bargain waiting for you to purchase and resell. Similarly, there is also an eager buyer waiting to purchase your property. The foundation of your personal wealth is built one transaction at a time.

PERSONAL FINANCIAL STATEMENT

For:___Your Name _____

Date: _____

Assets

Cash on hand_____

Checking _____

Savings _____

Real Estate Owned _____

Stocks _____

Individual Retirement Accounts _____

401(k) Plan _____

Certificates of Deposit_____

Accounts Receivable_____

Real Estate Notes Receivable _____

Cash Value Life Insurance _____

Office and Computer Equipment _____

Investment and Personal Jewelry _____

Investment Art and Antiques_____

Vehicles_____

Household Goods _____

Other: _____

Other: _____

Other: _____

TOTAL ASSETS: _____

Liabilities

Notes Payable _____

Accounts/Bills Due _____

Credit Cards Payable_____

Vehicle Loans _____

Unpaid Taxes_____

Real Estate Mortgages Payable_____

Land Contracts Payable _____

Loans Payable_____

Other: _____

Other: _____

TOTAL LIABILITES: _____

NET WORTH: _____
(Assets minus Liabilities)

MONTHLY INCOME
FROM ALL SOURCES: _____

ENDORSEMENTS

We first met Nolan Sluder in 1966. His guidance and teaching on investing in real estate and the use of creative financing have enabled us to achieve financial security for our future.

We bought our first house by using a diamond ring as a down payment. Later, we traded a motor home for two more houses. For more than thirty-eight years, we have bought and sold many properties. We have now achieved the goal of not being dependent upon Social Security for our retirement.

We recommend this book without reservation based upon our personal experience of following Nolan's plan for real estate investing.

Larry and Dollie Meade

We arrived in Tyler, Texas in May of 2001 to consult with Nolan Sluder about our financial security. During the many years we pastored churches, we did little to prepare ourselves for retirement.

Today we now own the home in which we live. We also own income-producing rental property and have sold several other properties for a profit. Needless to say, our financial statement now looks much better than it did just a few, short years ago.

Thank you, Nolan Sluder, for sharing your knowledge with us.

Paul and Jan Sluder

I'm a twenty-two-year-old pizza delivery boy who works for minimum wage. Just over a year ago, I received a tutorial from Mr. Sluder which contained the principles included in this book. This information guided me in the right direction in my real estate endeavors. I now own a four bedroom home (with no mortgage) and a duplex. I thank God for allowing me to meet up with Mr. Sluder who shared his knowledge of real estate with me.

Courtney Kelly

Real estate has always interested me. When I was a boy, my father owned and managed rental property. I learned many life lessons from him. However, I wanted more. Nolan Sluder administered a conference that really struck a chord in me to get busy. I am very thankful for his influence in my real estate business. The opportunities are there, and Mr. Sluder can equip you with the skills to seize them.

Samuel J. Priddy

As a woman in my early sixties who had recently left home and country to serve in missions, I was looking for ways to establish stable income for my future.

Real estate always seemed beyond my financial capacity. Nolan's training and personal help enabled me to buy a small, rental home below market value. It's reassuring to know I have a valuable, increasing, financial resource for my advancing years in missions.

Kaaren Robinson

We lost everything when my husband lost his job of twenty years. It was at that time we met Nolan Sluder. He helped us get into our first home. After living in it for one year, we sold the house for a profit. Our out-of-pocket expense for our next home was $400. Unheard of! Nolan helped restore our hope. We learned that we too could be millionaires. He convinced us TO START WITH WHAT WE HAD. Thank you, Nolan. May God bless the wisdom that you have poured into this book.

Phil and Magen Anderson

IMPORTANT
PRINCIPLES TO REMEMBER

- Real estate is the "crown jewel" of all investments.
- Start where you are with what you have.
- Income-producing real estate purchased at the right price is a safe haven for your money.
- What you pay for a property has nothing to do with what it is worth.
- You draw interest on both your investment and your profit when you use owner financing.
- Tenants pay for your rental property and give you a bonus for allowing them to do so.
- Equity growth is the wealth that accumulates while you sleep, rest, or go on vacation.
- Great fortunes are made and sustained through real estate.
- Never pay retail price for property you are buying to rent or resell.
- You make your money when you buy your bargain. It's better to buy a bad house in a good location than it is to buy a good house in a bad location.
- Do not depend on others to care for your needs as you grow older. Make your plans now to be financially self-sufficient.

NOW AVAILABLE!

More life-changing messages by Nolan Sluder, author of *Fix Your Social Security with Real Estate*

MONEY MANAGEMENT & WEALTH BUILDING THROUGH REAL ESTATE

In this six part seminar, Nolan Sluder shares practical steps of successful money management. You'll learn keys to buying and managing rental property, the secrets of owner financing, and the awesome truth that real estate is, indeed, the master wealth builder.

WOW! LOOK AT YOUR POTENTIAL!

In this three-hour series, Nolan Sluder teaches you to think the incredible, see the invisible, and do the impossible. You'll learn how to reverse negative thought patterns, see the possibilities all around you, and accomplish things you never thought possible.

To order these and other titles, visit ***www.nolansluder.com.***

TATE PUBLISHING, LLC

127 East Trade Centre Terrace
Mustang, Oklahoma 73064

(888) 361 - 9473

TATE PUBLISHING, LLC
www.tatepublishing.com